ANFERNEE (PENNY)
H A R D A W A Y

*(Photo on
front cover.)*

**Anfernee
Hardaway drives
around Derek
Harper of the
New York
Knicks.**

*(Photo on
previous pages.)*

**Hardaway slams
one over a
Washington
Bullets defender.**

Photography supplied by Wide World Photos Inc.

Library of Congress Cataloging-in-Publication Data
Rambeck, Richard.
Anfernee (Penny) Hardaway / Richard Rambeck
p. cm.
Summary: Surveys the basketball career of the young point guard
for the Orlando Magic, Penny Hardaway.
ISBN 1-56766-315-X (hard cover: lib. bdg.)

1. Hardaway, Anfernee --Juvenile literature. 2. Basketball
players --United States --Biography --Juvenile literature.
3. Orlando Magic (Basketball team) --Juvenile liturature.
[1. Hardaway, Anfernee. 2. Basketball players. 3. Afro-Americans
--Biography.]
I. Title.
GV884.H24R36   1996   96-14497
796.323'092 — dc20   CIP
[B]   AC

ANFERNEE (PENNY)
HARDAWAY

BY RICHARD RAMBECK

The Orlando Magic had high hopes for the 1995-96 season. After all, they had made it all the way to the league finals the year before, despite being one of the younger teams in the National Basketball Association. Led by gigantic center Shaquille O'Neal, Orlando was expected to be one of the top teams in the NBA in 1995-96. Then, disaster struck. In a preseason game against the Miami Heat, O'Neal drove for the basket and seemed ready to deliver a powerful dunk when Heat center Matt Geiger fouled him.

Geiger's foul damaged ligaments in O'Neal's thumb. Shaq was out for several weeks, missing the first 22 games of the regular season. Orlando had to play one-quarter of the season without the league's top 1994-95 scorer. So the Magic fell apart, right? Wrong. Orlando proved it had a lot more going for it than the seven-foot-one, 300-pound O'Neal. Soon, it was obvious that O'Neal wasn't the Magic's only great player. With Shaq out, guard Anfernee "Penny" Hardaway stepped up and became the star.

Hardaway averaged 27.0 points, 6.5 assists, and 5.8 rebounds a game while O'Neal was injured. Orlando went 17-5 without its starting center, and Hardaway was a major reason for the success. He was named the NBA's Player of the Month for November 1995, after helping Orlando to a 13-2 record that month. He

Hardaway goes to the basket for two points against the Cleveland Cavaliers.

scored a career-high 42 points in a game against New Jersey. In two other games, he hit the game-winning basket in the final seconds.

Hardaway, who was in only his third year of pro basketball, was already being compared with Chicago Bulls star Michael Jordan. "I'm proud to be compared to the greatest player ever," Hardaway said. Hardaway was a great scorer, a fine shooter, an excellent play-maker, and a good rebounder, and he could even block shots once in a while. At six-feet-seven, 207 pounds, he's bigger than most other point guards. In fact, Hardaway is big enough to play forward, but he's a point guard and the man who runs the Orlando offense.

Hardaway was already considered one of the top players in the NBA even before O'Neal got hurt. The Orlando guard was named to the All-NBA First Team after the 1994-95 season, joining such stars as Utah guard John Stockton, San Antonio center David Robinson, Chicago forward Scottie Pippen, and Utah forward Karl Malone. O'Neal, by the way, was picked to the Second Team. A year earlier, Hardaway had been named to the league's All-Rookie First Team.

In 1994-95, his second year in the NBA, Hardaway averaged 20.9 points, 7.2 assists, and 4.4 rebounds a game. He made 51.2 percent of his field goals and

Hardaway wins the NBA Rookie All-Star Game most valuable player trophy in 1994.

76.9 percent of his free throws. He also showed a nice touch from the three-point range, hitting 87 of 249 long-distance shots. Hardaway was picked to play for Dream Team III, the United States basketball team for the 1996 Summer Olympics in Atlanta. "I'm very excited," he said about the Olympics. "I'm also a little nervous."

Anfernee Deon Hardaway grew up in Memphis, Tennessee. He started playing basketball at a young age because that's what all the kids did in his neighborhood. Hardaway got his nickname from his grandmother. Sort of. His grandma called him "Pretty," as in "Pretty Baby."

However, because she had a thick Southern accent, his friends thought she was saying "Penny." The nickname stuck. "I would take 'Penny' over 'Pretty' any day," Hardaway said. "So I kept 'Penny' as a nickname."

Young Penny had a knack for basketball. His classmates in elementary school told him he'd play in the NBA some day. Penny didn't believe them. In fact, it wasn't until high school that he began to think he had any chance of getting to the NBA. When Hardaway finished high school, there wasn't a college team that didn't want him.. Hardaway chose to stay home and attend Memphis State University.

Hardaway frowns as he leaves the court after losing to the Boston Celtics.

Unfortunately, he couldn't play his freshman year at Memphis State because his grades and college test scores weren't high enough. It was a huge disappointment for Hardaway. He vowed to be a better student, and he made good on that promise. "A lot of people want to give up when times get rough," he said. "I've hung in there a lot of times, and that's gotten me to where I am now." Hardaway then played his sophomore and junior seasons for Memphis State before deciding to turn pro.

The NBA scouts loved Hardaway's all-around game and said he would be one of the top players picked in the 1993 draft. Hardaway had two tryouts with Orlando, which had the first pick in the draft. "The first time no one watched me," he said, figuring that the Magic weren't that interested in him. "The second time the executives of the organization watched me and were impressed." The Magic took Michigan star Chris Webber with the first pick, but the team wasn't planning to keep Webber. The team wanted Hardaway.

Golden State drafted Hardaway, and the stage was set for a deal between the two clubs. Orlando traded Webber to Golden State for Hardaway and three first-round draft picks. Hardaway had mixed emotions about the trade. On one hand, he was sad because he'd thought he

would be playing for Golden State. "But the happy part was that I got to go to Orlando, where I had wanted to go before the draft even started."The trade brought together two of the brightest young stars in the game—Hardaway and O'Neal.

In Hardaway's rookie year, the Magic made the playoffs and lost in the first round. In his second year, Orlando won its division, then defeated Boston in the first round, Chicago (and Michael Jordan) in the second round, and Indiana in the Eastern Conference finals. Although the Magic lost to Houston in the finals, four games to none, Hardaway and O'Neal served notice that the young Orlando team will be an NBA powerhouse for years to come.